Thirty-five Reasons Why I Keep The Bible Sabbath

by

Robert Franklin Correia

"A world without a Sabbath would be like a man without a smile, like a summer without flowers, and like a homestead without a garden. It is the joyous day of the whole week."

—Henry Ward Beecher

TEACH Services, Inc.
P U B L I S H I N G
www.TEACHServices.com

Copyright © 2005 R. S. Correia
Copyright revised © 2011 R. S. Correia
& TEACH Services, Inc.
ISBN-13: 978-1-57258-717-5 (Paperback)
ISBN-13: 978-1-57258-718-2 (Hardback)
ISBN-13: 978-1-57258-719-9 (ePub)
ISBN-13: 978-1-57258-756-4 (Kindle)
Library of Congress Control Number: 2011937760

Published by

TEACH Services, Inc.
P U B L I S H I N G
www.TEACHServices.com

Dedicated to

My wife Reva

My children
Alyse, Carlos, Don and Bob

Foreword I

Robert Correia was very interested in science and religion. Whenever you were in his presence, whether the occasion was spelunking or hunting fossils on the banks of the James River, he exuded a confidence in the compatibility of science and Scripture. In 1992 Correia authored a most interesting work titled *Correlation of Science and The Scripture*. This book glitters with examples of his study, knowledge, and observance of nature. It also is a brilliant correlation of the Bible record and what he observed in God's beautiful creation.

Knowing Robert Correia as a personal friend was a great privilege for me. So it is now an honor for me to recommend *The Bible Sabbath* for your study and reading. In this work, Correia has meticulously given 35 very interesting reasons for his observance of the Bible Sabbath. You will find his historical biblical approach not only factual but very convincing.

As you, dear reader, explore these 35 reasons for keeping the Bible Sabbath, I feel certain that you will be impressed as I have been that Robert Correia has brought to our attention very convincing evidence from his methodical research and comparison of Bible texts proving that the seventh day (Saturday) is the true Bible Sabbath.

Dr. Richard Bendall
President, World Health Services
July 2003

Foreword II

Having read these pages of *The Bible Sabbath*, I am happy to write this foreword. The subject of the Sabbath is vital to the Christian, for only he whose sins have been forgiven through the grace of Jesus Christ can enter into the "rest" of God. "The wicked . . . cannot rest," declares the prophet Isaiah, while Jesus cried with outstretched arms, "Come unto Me . . . and I will give you rest." This is the eternal purpose of the gospel. And yet there are many who, loving the Lord, are confused on this great question.

I feel Robert Correia has made a splendid contribution to this great subject. The arguments he has presented from the Word of God are clear and irrefutable, while the many quotations from history reveal a deep research. My association with the writer in the classroom has led me to appreciate his thorough work while my personal esteem for him has urged me to a careful examination of this presentation of the Sabbath question. Now as it goes forth on its mission, I sincerely pray that He whose mighty Word spoke creation into existence will speak again through the truth of the written Word of God and that His Holy Spirit will banish the darkness of ignorance and reveal His finished creation in the hearts of those who read.

R. Allan Anderson
La Sierra University
June 1939

Introduction

"Come now, and let us reason together" (Isa. 1:18). In our investigation of the true Bible Sabbath, our appeal is not made to great logic, judicial powers, or profound discernment, but to reason. In all sincerity this seems the best way, the Bible way, and the only fair way of dealing with this important subject. In the words of the Bible we repeat: "Let us REASON together."

Since the Bible and the Bible only is the Christian's guide; since "all scripture . . . is profitable for doctrine, for reproof, for correction, for instruction in righteousness: that the man of God may be perfect, *thoroughly furnished* unto *all* good works" (2 Tim. 3:16, 17); since God's holy Word is the truth, the whole truth, and nothing but the truth (John 17:17); surely it does reveal the truth concerning the true Bible Sabbath. Therefore, we appeal to the Bible as the standard of our inquiry. The Holy Scriptures will be the rule of judgment, the court of appeal in our investigation of the true Bible Sabbath.

Throughout the book the author has used italicization of key words for emphasis.

Robert Franklin Correia

Thirty-five Reasons
Why I keep the Bible Sabbath

I keep the Bible Sabbath:

1. **Because God Himself kept the Bible Sabbath.**

God made a sufficient proof of His regard for the true Sabbath by resting the very first seventh day after the creation of this earth:

Since:

- "He [God] rested on the seventh day" (Gen. 2:2).
- "On the seventh day he [God] rested" (Ex. 31:17).
- "The LORD blessed the sabbath [seventh] day" (Ex. 20:11).
- "God did rest the seventh day" (Heb. 4:4).

Whereas:

- "The seventh day is the sabbath" (Ex. 20:10).
- "The seventh day is the sabbath" (Lev. 23:3).
- "The seventh day is the sabbath" (Deut. 5:14).
- "The seventh [day] is the sabbath" (Ex. 31:15).
- "The seventh day, which is the sabbath" (Ex. 16:26).

Therefore:

- It is as plain as day the Bible teaches that God Himself kept the seventh-day Sabbath.

My first reason for keeping the Bible Sabbath is sufficient in itself to settle the whole question now and forevermore—God Himself kept the seventh-day Sabbath. That is conclusive evidence to substantiate and vindicate my keeping, your keeping, or anyone else's keeping of the seventh-day Sabbath. Who could be wrong or even be accused of doing wrong when they follow the example of God Himself in keeping the very Sabbath day that God kept.

2. Because God instituted it at Creation for us to keep.

"Thus the heavens and the earth were finished, and all the host of them. And on the seventh day God ended his work which he had made; and he rested on the seventh day from all his work which He had made. And God *blessed* the seventh day, and *sanctified* it: because that in it he had rested from all his work which God created and made" (Gen. 2:1-3).

"For in six days the LORD made heaven and earth, the sea, and all that in them is, and rested the seventh day: wherefore the LORD *blessed* the sabbath day, and *hallowed* it" (Ex. 20:11).

- God *blessed* the seventh day (Gen. 2:1-3).
- The Lord *blessed* the Sabbath day (Ex. 20:11).
- God *sanctified* the seventh day (Gen. 2:1-3).
- The Lord *hallowed* the Sabbath day (Ex. 20:11).

Please notice that God *blessed* and *sanctified* the seventh-day Sabbath at the end of Creation. The blessing and sanctification show it was instituted at that time for humanity to keep.

"God *blessed* the seventh day" (Gen. 2:3). God has said: "I change not" (Mal. 3:6), and in Him there "is no variableness, neither shadow of turning" (James 1:17). Consequently, when God blesses anything, the blessing cannot be *reversed* (Num. 23:20), because when God *blesses* anything, it "shall be *blessed for ever*" (1 Chron. 17:27).

"God ... *sanctified* **it"** (Gen. 2:3; see also Ex. 20:8-11). According to Webster's dictionary "sanctify" means "to set apart to holy use." The Bible states: "And God blessed the seventh day, and sanctified it: *because* that in it he *had* rested." This shows that the day had already passed before He blessed and sanctified it; therefore, He blessed and sanctified the seventh days then future, answering to the seventh day that had just passed on which He *had* rested.

The above evidence clearly demonstrates the fact that God Himself has attached the utmost importance to the seventh-day Sabbath by His personal blessing and sanctification, thereby definitely fixing the seventh day for all time as the only and true Sabbath.

God is the giver of rest, for He says to all, "Come unto me... and I will give you rest" (Matt. 11:28; see also Ex. 33:14). God knows what is the right day on which to rest, and He has given humanity the seventh-day Sabbath as a day of rest:

- "The seventh day thou shalt rest" (Ex. 23:12; 34:21).
- "The seventh [day] is the sabbath of rest" (Ex. 31:15).
- "The seventh day is the sabbath of rest" (Lev. 23:3).

God appointed the seventh day as a Sabbath, a day of rest from secular work because He Himself had rested from all His work. God's rest was not made necessary by fatigue (Isa. 40:28), but He rested on that day as an example to all people, thus making His rest on the seventh day a reason why we should rest on the seventh day—that we should do as God had done. Notice the following texts that prove that God rested on the seventh day:

- God "rested on the seventh day" (Gen. 2:2).
- "On the seventh day he [God] rested" (Ex. 31:17).
- God "rested the seventh day". (Ex. 20:11).
- "God did rest the seventh day" (Heb. 4:4).

It is no wonder that in the New Testament after Jesus' death on the cross the followers of Christ "*rested* the sabbath day according to the commandment" (Luke 23:56). No wonder the book of Hebrews in the New Testament positively states: "There remaineth therefore a *rest* [keeping of a Sabbath] to the people of God.... Let us labour therefore to enter into that *rest*, lest any man fall after the same example of unbelief" (Heb. 4:9-11).

So, we can see that the seventh-day Sabbath is not man-made but God-made. It is not only the oldest institution but also the first institution that God gave to man, being older and as significant as the marriage institution. Since the setting apart of the seventh day as the Sabbath day was coincident with the *origin* of man, the observance of that seventh day as the Sabbath is to be coexistent and coextensive with the *duration* of humanity.

3. Because the Sabbath was made for humanity.

Jesus said: "The sabbath was made for *man*" (Mark 2:27). Man in this text means human being, mankind (cf. Webster; see also Matt. 4:4; John 1:9).

The Bible does *not* say: "The Sabbath was made for the Jew." It says: "The sabbath was made for *man*" (Mark 2:27). It also says: "The woman [was made] for the *man*" (1 Cor. 11:9).

How could the Sabbath be made for the Jew only when it was instituted at Creation (Gen. 2:1-3; Ex. 20:8-11)—2,500 years before a Jew existed? A Jew is "a descendant of Judah," according to *Young's Analytical Concordance.*

Notice the Sabbath commandment itself: "Remember the sabbath day, to keep it holy…. the seventh day is the sabbath of the LORD thy God [not Jew]: in it thou shalt not do any work, thou, nor thy son, nor thy daughter, thy manservant, nor thy maidservant, nor thy cattle, nor *thy stranger* that is within thy gates" (Ex. 20:8-10). Please tell us to whom *thy stranger* refers if it does not refer to someone who is not a Jew. God took the most scrupulous precautions against such an idea by writing into the fourth commandment the term *thy stranger*, who is not a *Jew* (cf. Ex. 12:49; Num. 15:16, 29; Isa. 56:6-8).

Those who contend that the Sabbath was made *only* for the Jew will, by the force of their own consistency, have to admit that the woman was also made *only* for the Jew and the Jew is the only man who can have a wife, because the woman was made for the same *man* for whom the Sabbath was made. The Sabbath was given the same time marriage was given, and it applies to all people the same as marriage applies. So we can see plainly that the Sabbath is no more exclusively for the Jew than is the marriage institution. The Sabbath is not man-made but God-made, and it was made for all individuals across the world for all time.

"'Twas set apart before the fall,
'Twas made for man, 'twas made for all."
(R. F. Cottrell).

4. Because God commanded man to keep the Sabbath.

Notice how many times the Bible repeats God's command for people to keep the Sabbath:

- "Remember the sabbath day, to *keep* it holy" (Ex. 20:8).
- "Verily my sabbaths ye shall *keep*" (Ex. 31:13).
- "Ye shall *keep* my sabbaths" (Lev. 19:30; 26:2).
- "*Keep* the sabbath day" (Deut. 5:12).
- "*Keep* my sabbaths" (Lev. 19:3).

What stronger language could be used? The Sabbath that most people are forgetting, that very Sabbath, God says to "*remember*." God knew that people would forget His Sabbath. No wonder the fourth commandment, which deals with the Sabbath, is the only one of all God's holy Ten Commandments that begins with the word "*remember*."

"*Remember* the sabbath day to keep it holy. Six days shalt thou labour, and do all thy work: but *the seventh day is the sabbath of the LORD thy God*: In it thou shalt not do any work" (Ex. 20:8-10).

5. Because God commands us to keep not *a* day but *the seventh day*.

God does not say in His commandment that humanity is to keep *a* seventh day or *any* seventh day or *your* seventh day. Nor did God say to keep the day of Christ's birth or the day of Christ's death or the day of Christ's resurrection. The *only* weekly day that God or the Bible definitely and distinctly commanded should be kept is *"the seventh day* [which] *is the sabbath of the LORD thy God"* (Ex. 20:10). How grandly simple the Bible makes this in the following texts:

- *The seventh day* God ended His work (Gen. 2:2.
- *The seventh day* God rested (Gen 2:2).
- *The seventh day* God blessed (Gen. 2:3).
- *The seventh day* God sanctified (Gen. 2:3).

- *The seventh day* God had rested (Gen. 2:3).
- *The seventh day* God told us to remember (Ex. 20:8).
- *The seventh day* God made the Sabbath day (Ex. 20:8).
- *The seventh day* God made holy (Ex. 20:8; Isa. 58:13).
- *The seventh day* God told us to refrain from work (Ex. 20:10).
- *The seventh day* God made His Sabbath (Ex. 20:10).
- *The seventh day* God rested (Ex. 20:11).
- *The seventh day* God blessed (Ex. 20:11).

The seventh day God hallowed (Ex. 20:11).

There is only one Independence Day—only one right day to celebrate the Fourth of July—so it is with the Sabbath—*the seventh day* is the *only right Sabbath day* for people to keep. Therefore, every seventh day Sabbath should be underscored with red because it is God's red-letter day of the week—the best day of the week!

6. Because the seventh-day Sabbath is the *Lord's day*.

All through the Bible we are repeatedly told that the Lord has a definite and special day. The Lord's regard for the Lord's day is stressed in terms of possession. For example, to show possession of my hat, I would say "Correia's hat; hat of Correia; or my hat." In the same way, the Lord shows His possession of His day by calling it "The Lord's day; day of the Lord; or My day." Notice the following texts:

- "The *Lord's day*" (Rev. 1:10).
- "*Lord* even of the sabbath *day*" (Matt. 12:8).
- "*Lord* also of the sabbath" (Mark 2:28; Luke 6:5).
- "My holy *day*" (Isa. 58:13; see also Neh. 9:14; Ex. 31:15; Lev. 19:3, 30).

15

- "The seventh *day* is the sabbath of the *LORD*" (Ex. 20:10).
- "The seventh *day* is the sabbath of the *LORD*" (Deut. 5:14; see also Lev. 23:3).

Who can doubt the plain statement of the Holy Bible when it gives all these scriptural witnesses to testify that the seventh-day Sabbath is the Lord's day?

7. **Because the Sabbath is the *sign* between God and His people forever.**

As most items have a particular brand or trademark attached to it to establish their genuineness, as every police officer has a badge to indicate their authority, as every official has a seal to ascertain their identification and power, so God has a visible mark or sign between Him and His people that forever distinguishes them. The Bible plainly states what this sign is:

- "I gave them my *sabbaths*, to be a *sign* between me and them" (Eze. 20:12).
- "Hallow my *sabbaths*; and they shall be a *sign* between me and you" (Eze. 20:20).
- "My *sabbaths* ye shall keep: for it is a *sign* between me and you" (Ex. 31:13).
- "It is a *sign* between me and the children of Israel *for ever*" (Ex. 31:17).

8. **Because the Sabbath is God's flag.**

God has a flag:

- "I [God] will set up My *ensign*" (Isa. 49:22, RV).

A flag is a sign:

- "They set up their *ensigns for signs*" (Ps. 74:4).

God's sign is His Sabbath:

- "I gave them my sabbaths, to be a *sign*" (Eze. 20:12; see also verse 20).
- "It [my Sabbath] is a *sign*" (Ex. 31:13).
- "It [my Sabbath] is a *sign...*for ever" (Ex. 31:17).

Since God has a flag (Isa. 49:22, RV), and a flag is a sign (Ps. 74:4), and God's sign is His Sabbath (Eze. 20:12, 20), therefore, God's *flag is His Sabbath*, because things equal to the same things are equal to each other.

God took of the fabric of time and made Himself an ensign for eternity. He made a unit of time by the rolling of a globe, and He called that unit day. He took a handful of days—seven—and made them a week. And of that week He took the last day, the seventh, and made it the Sabbath. That Sabbath is His sign, His emblem, His *flag*.

A flag is more than a mere piece of cloth. It is a special piece of cloth consecrated to the definite purpose of signifying all that a government is and has. So is the Sabbath. It is more than merely a day. It is a special day. Like the cloth in a flag it is a piece of time that has a special significance, being consecrated by God Himself to represent the government of God with all its power, purpose, and privilege. The Sabbath, therefore, is as different from any other day as the flag is different from any piece of cloth.

Since the Sabbath is the flag of God's kingdom and I am a subject of God's kingdom, I want to see the *home flag* flutter because it speaks of the homeland. Just as Old Glory has gathered people out of all nations to America and is a sign of America, so God's flag reminds us that we are strangers and pilgrims in a foreign land (Heb. 11:13)—our home is far away upon a golden strand.

The Sabbath is God's flag all the way from paradise lost to paradise regained, and under God's flag He will finally rally the faithful who will be gathered from earth's remotest bounds (Isa. 11:12). Just as no flag could take the place of Old Glory to the true American, so it is that no other day could take the place of God's seventh-day Sabbath to the true Christian. Any flag won't do; neither will any day do. It is nothing short of high treason to disrespect God's flag. Men have too long scuffed God's flag under their feet. It is high time to rally round the flag of God and let it wave as our standard forever. At any cost we must be as loyal to and true to God's flag as Barbara Frietchie was to the Stars and Stripes when she stated: "Shoot, if you must, this old gray head, But spare your country's flag."

9. Because God brought Israel out of Egypt in order to preserve His Sabbath, a parallel to the final redemption of humanity.

When Moses endeavored to persuade the Israelites to keep the Sabbath in Egypt, Pharaoh made a law against it (Ex. 5:5-9).

Therefore God took Israel out of Egypt to keep the Sabbath: "Keep the sabbath day to sanctify it ... the seventh day is the sabbath of the LORD thy God: in it thou shalt not do any work ... And *remember* that thou was a servant in the land of Egypt, and that the LORD thy God brought thee out thence through a *mighty hand* and by a stretched out arm: *therefore*

the LORD thy God *commanded* thee to *keep the sabbath day*"
(Deut. 5:12-15; cf. Ps. 105:43-45).

We have every assurance that the Sabbath will play a
prominent part in the final redemption of humanity in a manner that will be similar to the parallel to the Exodus. Notice the
unmistakable evidence from the Bible:

"And in *that day* there shall be a root of Jesse, which shall
stand for an *ensign* [cf. No. 8] of the people; to it shall the Gentiles seek: and his *rest* [cf. Ex. 16:23; Heb. 4:9, margin] shall
be glorious. And it shall come to pass in *that day*, that the Lord
shall set his hand again the *second time to recover the remnant
of his people* [first time at the Exodus, Deut. 5:12-15] ... And
he shall set up an *ensign* [cf No. 8] for the nations, and shall as-
semble the outcasts of Israel, and gather together the dispersed
of Judah from the four corners of the earth" (Isa. 11:10-12).

10. Because at least fifteen days before Sinai God reproved His people for not keeping the seventh-day Sabbath (Ex. 16:1; 19:1).

Since so many falsely believe that the Sabbath command
did not exist before Sinai, this reason and proof is of profound
significance to the sincere seeker of Bible truth. Notice the
Bible evidence that shows that the Sabbath command existed
before Sinai:

- "How long refuse ye to *keep my commandments and
  my laws*? See, for that the LORD hath given you the
  sabbath" (Ex. 16:28, 29; cf. verse 4).
- "This is that which the LORD hath said, To morrow is
  the rest of the holy sabbath" (Ex. 16:23).

This scriptural evidence that shows that the Sabbath commandment was in existence before Sinai is highly credible, open, aboveboard, and explicit. Notice the following lessons God taught His people that day concerning the Sabbath:

- What day it is (Ex. 16:26).
- What it is (Ex. 16:23).
- How to prepare for it (Ex. 16:23, 26).
- How it should be kept (Ex. 16:30).
- With what it is associated (Ex. 16:28).
- Who gave it to them (Ex. 16:29).

11. Because the Ten Commandment law that contains the Sabbath commandment will stand *forever and ever*.

"The works of his hands are verity and judgment; all his *commandments* are sure. They *stand fast for ever and ever*" (Ps. 111:7, 8; cf. 119:152).

To prove that "his commandments" in this quotation refer to the Ten Commandments, which contains the Sabbath, we call to your attention the expression *"works of his hands."* The only commandments that were the works of God's hands—and in fact the only thing that God ever wrote with His own hands according to the Bible—are the Ten Commandments. Notice the following text:

"He commanded you to perform, even *ten commandments*; and he *wrote them* upon two tables of stone" (Deut. 4:13; cf. Ex. 31:18; 34:1).

12. Because God would *not change His law* and He forbade humanity to change it.

God would not change it: "I am the LORD, I change not" (Mal. 3:6).

God forbade humanity to change it: "Ye *shall not add* unto the word which I *command* you, neither shall ye *diminish* ought from it, that ye may keep the *commandments* of the LORD" (Deut. 4:2; cf. 12:32).

Christ taught that the law remained unchanged: "Do not for a moment suppose that I have come to *abrogate the Law...* Solemnly I tell you that until Heaven and earth pass away, *not one iota or smallest detail will pass away from the Law* until all has taken place" (Matt. 5:17, 18, WNT).

Paul, James, and John taught that the law remained unchanged: "Do we then make void the law through faith? God forbid: yea we *establish the law*" (Rom. 3:31). "The *doers of the law* shall be justified" (Rom. 2:13).

"If ye fulfill the royal law ... *ye do well* ... For whosoever shall keep the *whole law*, and yet offend in *one point*, he is guilty of all" (James 2:8-12; cf. 1 John 2:4-6; 5:3).

13. Because anyone who attempts to *change God's law,* which contains the Sabbath commandment, is *against God.*

For anyone to attempt to change God's holy law, it would seem to the true Christian like the touch of a profane hand upon the ark of God. Through all the history of the world God has maintained the laissez-faire theory in regard to His law—"Let well enough alone." In spite of this, fools rush in where angels fear to tread, and people have attempted to change God's law. Notice what the Bible states concerning this high treason:

"And he shall speak great words *against the most High,* and ... think to *change times and laws*" (Dan. 7:25).

"The earth also is defiled under the inhabitants thereof; because they have *transgressed* the laws, *changed* the ordinance, *broken* the everlasting [Ex. 31:16] covenant" (Isa. 24:5; cf. Zeph. 3:1-4; Eze. 22:26).

14. Because God is *against* those who are *against* His law, which contains the Sabbath commandment.

"Therefore as the fire devoureth the stubble ... so their root shall be as rottenness ... because they have *cast away the law of the LORD*" (Isa. 5:24).

"Whosoever therefore shall break *one* of these least commandments, and shall teach men so, he shall be called the *least* in the kingdom of heaven" (Matt. 5:19).

"He that turneth away his ear from hearing the *law*, even his *prayer shall be abomination*" (Prov. 28:9; cf. Hosea 4:6; Isa. 30:9; Jer. 6:19).

15. Because the law which contains the Sabbath contains the same great eternal qualities of God Himself.

The *close relationship* existing between God and His law is demonstrated below to a mathematical nicety:

God is:	His law is:
Righteous (Ps. 145:17)	Righteous (Ps. 119:172)
Love	Based on love
(1 John 4:8, 16)	(Matt. 22:36-40)
Holy (Lev. 11:44)	Holy (Rom. 7:12)
Spirit (John 4:24)	Spiritual (Rom. 7:14)
Perfect (Matt. 5:48)	Perfect (Ps. 19:7; James 1:25)
God of truth (Ps. 31:5)	Truth (Mal. 2:6)

God is:	His law is:
God of peace (Rom. 16:20)	Peace through (Ps. 119:165; Isa. 48:18)
Unchangeable (Ps. 111:7, 8)	Unchangeable (Ps. 89:34-37; Matt. 5:17-19)

God's law manifests His qualities to such an extent that He Himself identifies Himself with His law by calling it the *"royal law"* (James 2:8-12).

16. Because the law, which contains the Sabbath, *is the standard* by which *true and false* religions are determined.

"To the law and to the testimony: if they speak not according to this word, it is because *there is no light in them"* (Isa. 8:20).

17. Because the law, which contains the Sabbath, will be *the standard* by which God's final judgment will be made.

It is a cold fact; nevertheless, it is as true as the needle is to the pole that God's law, which contains His Sabbath, will be the standard of His judgment. Notice the following biblical evidence for this claim:

- *"Judged by the law"* (Rom 2:12).
- *"Judged by the law* of liberty" (James 2:8-13; cf. Eccl. 12:12, 13).

18. Because the *law of God* in the Scriptures is very carefully distinguished from the *Law of Moses*, which expired at the cross.

God spoke the Ten Commandment law with His *own* voice and wrote it with His *own* finger upon tables of stone (Deut. 4:12, 13); therefore, there is no excuse for anyone to be so misinformed as to say that Moses gave and wrote the Ten Commandment law.

The Law of Moses is as carefully separated from the law of God in the Holy Bible as the North Pole is from the South Pole. I have taken the time to trace though the entire Bible from beginning to end, Genesis to Revelation, and I have found scores of passages that mention these two laws, but never are they confused. On the contrary, the Bible carefully, clearly, and plainly distinguishes between the law of God and the Law of Moses, showing they are two separate and distinct laws. When the Bible separates these two laws, it is a good policy for us as humans to do the same.

What the Constitution is to the United States, so God's holy Ten Commandment law is to His government. America may make covenants, codes, ordinances, and statutes, but never should we repeal or change the Constitution, which is our basic law. The Law of Moses likewise contained codes, contracts, pledges, ordinances, and rites, which were given and taken away, but not God's holy basic Ten Commandment law. It never was, is, or will be changed or repealed. How could God repeal such commandments as thou shalt not steal, murder, kill, etc.? Right in the very heart of such basic commandments is found the seventh-day Sabbath commandment. No wonder the Bible tells us that "until Heaven and earth pass away, *not one iota or smallest detail will pass away from the Law* until all has taken place" (Matt. 5:18, WNT).

That the law of God is carefully separated from the Law of Moses in the Scriptures will be demonstrated beyond all possibility of successful contradiction in the following table:

Law of God	Law of Moses
Called royal law (James 2:8)	Called law contained in ordinances (Eph. 2:15)
Spoken by God (Deut. 4:12)	Spoken by Moses (Lev. 1:1-3)
Written by God (Deut. 4:13)	Handwriting of ordinances (Col. 2:14)
Written by God's finger (Ex. 31:18)	Written by Moses (2 Chron. 35:12)
Written on tables of stone (Ex. 24:12)	Written in a book (2 Chron. 35:12)
Placed in ark (Ex. 40:20)	Placed in side of ark (Deut. 31:24-26)
Is perfect (Ps. 19:7)	Made nothing perfect (Heb. 7:19)
Stands fast forever and ever (Ps. 111:7, 8)	Nailed to cross (Col. 2:14)
Was not destroyed by Christ (Matt. 5:17-19)	Was abolished by Christ (Eph. 2:15)
Magnified by Christ (Isa. 42:21)	Taken out of way by Christ (Col. 2:14)
Gives knowledge of sin (Rom. 3:20; 7:7)	Instituted in consequence of sin (Lev. 4:7)

19. Because the patriarchs kept the Ten Commandment law which contains the seventh-day Sabbath.

"Abraham ... *kept my charge, my commandments* ... and *my laws*" (Gen. 26:5; cf. Gen. 4:3 margin).

Some seem to think the Ten Commandment law of God's law was not in existence before Sinai. The above text shows such an objection is not an explanation but merely an excuse— a self-evident falsity. Such an opinion runs counter to facts. To those who question the existence of the Ten Commandments in the *patriarchal age* we submit the following:

- First commandment (Gen. 31:30; Joshua 24:2)

- Second commandment (Gen. 31:19; 35:4.)
- Third commandment (2 Peter 2:7, 8)
- Fourth commandment (Gen. 2:1-3; 4:3 margin)
- Fifth commandment (Gen. 9:20-25; 27:19, 24; 37:31-35)
- Sixth commandment (Gen. 4:8-13; 9:5, 6)
- Seventh commandment (Gen. 34:2; 35:22; 38:18; 39:7-10)
- Eighth commandment (Gen. 30:33; 31:19; 44:8)
- Ninth commandment (Gen. 20:2-12; 27:19, 24; 50:15-17)
- Tenth commandment (Gen. 3:6; 37:11)

20. **Because the Bible writers themselves, by precept and example, admonish the true Christian to *keep the law*.**

- Abraham: "Kept … my commandments" (Gen. 26:5).
- Moses: "Remember the *sabbath day,* to *keep* it holy" (Ex. 20:8).
- Nehemiah: "*Keep* my commandments" (Neh. 1:9; see also 9:13, 14).
- Job: "*Receive* … the law" (Job 22:22).
- David: "I shall *keep* thy law" (Ps. 119:34; see also verses 119:44, 55; 78:1).
- Solomon: "Whoso *keepeth* the law is a wise son" (Prov. 28:7; see also 29:18).
- Isaiah: "Blessed is the man … that *keepeth* the sabbath" (Isa. 56:2).
- Ezekiel: "They shall *keep* my laws and … hallow my sabbaths" (Eze. 44:24).
- Daniel: "*Keep* his commandments" (Dan. 9:4).
- Matthew: "*Keep* the commandments" (Matt. 19:17).

- John: "He that hath my commandments, and keepeth them, he … loveth me" (John 14:21).
- Paul: "*Keeping* of the commandments" (1 Cor. 7:19; see also Rom. 3:31; 7:6, 7).
- James: "*Keep* the whole law" (James 2:10).
- Christ's church: "*Keep* the commandments" (Rev. 12:17; 14:12).
- Passport into heaven: "*Do* his commandments" (Rev. 22:14).
- Angels: "Angels … *do* his commandments" (Ps. 103:20).
- Jesus: "I have *kept* my Father's commandments" (John 15:10).
- Christ said: "If ye love me, *keep* my commandments" (John 14:15); "*Keep* the commandments" (Matt. 19:17).

Please notice the sum and substance—conclusion—of the whole matter as stated by the Bible itself: "Let us hear the *conclusion* of the whole matter: Fear God, and *keep his commandments: for this is the whole duty* of man" (Eccl. 12:13).

21. Because the *Ten Commandment law* or *law of God*, which contains the seventh-day Sabbath, is endorsed by the New Testament.

Some seem to think the New Testament does not endorse the Ten Commandments. Upon what grounds are such decisions based? The facts bear sufficient witness to prove beyond all reasonable doubt or question that the New Testament, as shown below, not only endorses the Ten Commandments, the fourth of which is the seventh-day Sabbath, but repeats many of them verbatim.

The New Testament Decalogue

I

"Thou shalt worship the Lord thy God, and him only shalt thou serve" (Matt. 4:10; see also 22:37).

II

"Little children, keep yourselves from idols" (1 John 5:21). "Forasmuch then as we are the offspring of God, we ought not to think that the Godhead is like unto gold, or silver, or stone, graven by art and man's device" (Acts 17:29; see also John 4:24).

III

"That the name of God and his doctrine be not blasphemed" (1 Tim. 6:1; see also Matt. 5:33-37; James 5:12).

IV

"Pray ye that your flight be not in the winter, *neither on the sabbath day*" (Matt. 24:20). "The sabbath was made for man, and not man for the sabbath: Therefore the Son of man is Lord also of the sabbath" (Mark 2:27, 28). "For he spake in a certain place of the seventh day on this wise, And God did rest the seventh day from all His works" (Heb. 4:4). "There remaineth therefore a rest [keeping of a Sabbath] to the people of God. For he that is entered into his rest, he also hath ceased from his own works, as God did from his" (verses 9, 10). "For by him were all things created, that are in heaven, and that are in earth" (Col. 1:16; see also Matt. 28:1; Luke 4:16; 23:54, 56).

V

"Honour thy father and thy mother" (Matt. 19:19; see also Matt. 15:4-9; Eph. 6:1-3; Luke 18:20).

VI

"Thou shalt not kill" (Rom. 13:9; Matt. 5:21, 22; 1 John 3:15; James 2:10-12).

VII

"Thou shalt not commit adultery" (Matt. 19:18; see also Matt. 5:27, 28; Rom. 13:9; Luke 18:20; James 2:10-12).

VIII

"Thou shalt not steal" (Rom. 13:9; see also Matt. 19:18; 15:19; Mark 10:19; Luke 18:20).

IX

"Thou shalt not bear false witness" (Rom. 13:9; see also Matt. 19:18; Mark 10:19; Luke 18:20).

X

"Thou shalt not covet" (Rom 7:7; see also Matt. 19:21, 22; Rom. 13:9).

22. **Because Jesus Christ identifies Himself in close relationship with the Ten Commandment law that contains the Sabbath.**

The following evidence is not only richly suggestive but

affords striking testimony in favor of the seventh-day Sabbath law.

- Christ came not to destroy the law (Matt. 5:17).
- Christ testifies to the perpetuity of the law (Matt. 5:17-19).
- Christ came to "magnify the law, and make it honourable" (Isa. 42:21).
- Christ kept His "Father's commandments" (John 15:10).
- Christ is our example. We are to do as He did and observe what He observed (1 Peter 2:21; 1 John 2:6).
- Christ said, "If thou wilt enter into life, *keep the [ten] commandments*" (Matt. 19:17).

Note: I wish to stress the fact that by their association together in the Bible, the New Testament as well as the Old Testament, the words *law* and *commandment* are interchangeable and have the same meaning (See Gen. 26:5; Ex. 16:28; 24:12; 1 Kings 2:3; 2 Kings 17:37; 2 Chron. 14:4; 19:10; 31:21; Ezra 10:3; Neh. 9:13, 29, 34; Prov. 3:1; Matt. 19:17, 18; Luke 18:20; Rom. 13:8, 9; James 2:8-10).

23. Because the *new commandment* of Christ leads me to keep the Sabbath.

The new commandment is worthy of attentive study and careful consideration. Here is Christ's new commandment: "That ye love one another" (John 13:34; 15:12; see also 1 John 3:23; 4:21). Far be it from me to give any one the impression that I believe the new commandment does away with God's Ten Commandments because it does not according to the Bible. Notice what the new commandment leads the true Christian to do:

"Not as though I wrote a *new commandment* unto thee, but that which *we had from the beginning,* that *we love on another.* And *this is love,* that we walk *after his commandments*" (2 John 5, 6).

"We know that we love the children of God, when we love God, and *keep his commandments.* For *this is the love of God,* that we *keep his commandments:* and *his commandments* are not grievous" (1 John 5:2, 3).

Jesus Himself did not teach that the new commandment was the *only* commandment that we should keep. Christ said, "If ye love me, *keep my commandments*" (John 14:15).

Of which commandments did Jesus speak? "Which? Jesus said, Thou shalt do no murder, Thou shalt not commit adultery, Thou shalt not steal, Thou shalt not bear false witness, Honour thy father and thy mother: and Thou shalt love thy neighbour as thyself" (Matt. 19:18, 19).

These commandments are contained in the Ten Commandments, which also contain the Sabbath. In this passage Jesus did not command the keeping of any of the first four commandments. Is that any reason for people to break them? Is that any reason for people to worship idols, curse God, or break God's Sabbath? Is the *silence* of God's New Testament servants in the valleys of Judea more weighty than the *thunderings* of God Himself on Mount Sinai? The answer is no. These with the other four are the commandments of which Jesus was speaking when He said: "If thou wilt enter into life, keep the commandments" (Matt. 19:17; cf. Ex. 20:1-17).

Since God is love (1 John 4:8) and the whole gospel is

based on love (1 Cor. 13), since Jesus has said, "If ye love me, keep my commandments" (John 14:15), we understand that love is the basic factor of Christianity and that Jesus, the founder of Christianity, stresses love in His new commandment. No wonder the new commandment, which is the real essence of the whole Ten Commandments, was given. This agrees with the following text: "Love is the fulfilling [*pleroma*, Greek for fullness] of the law" (Rom. 13:10).

The following quote by D. L. Moody appears in *Bible Readings for the Home Circle*, page 392:

1. Love to God will admit no other God.
2. Love will not debase the object it adores.
3. Love to God will never dishonor His name.
4. Love to God will reverence His day.
5. Love to parents will honor them.
6. Hate, not love, is a murderer.
7. Lust, not love, commits adultery.
8. Love will give, but never steal.
9. Love will not slander nor lie.
10. Love's eye is not covetous.

Thus it is as clear as day that love or Christ's new commandments does not do away with the Ten Commandments but establishes them because: "Love is the *fulfilling of the law*" (Rom. 13:10).

24. Because Jesus Christ the Son of God *kept the seventh-day Sabbath* all His life.

If anyone would know which was the right Sabbath day to keep, surely it would be Jesus Christ, the Son of God, and He kept the seventh-day Sabbath all His life: "*As his custom was, he* [Jesus] went into the synagogue [church] on the *sabbath day* ... and taught them on the *sabbath days*" (Luke 4:16, 31).

The custom of the world is not the custom of Jesus. The custom of the world causes people to keep any day, but the custom of Jesus causes us to keep *the* Sabbath day—the very day that Jesus' Father kept at Creation (Gen. 2:1-3). If it was good enough for Jesus, it is good enough for me. I am confident of one thing and of this thing there can be no doubt or question: It was the *custom of Jesus to go to church on the Sabbath day*.

The Bible mentions that Jesus attended the following churches:

* Capernaum church (Mark 1:21).
* Nazareth church (Luke 4:16).

The Bible also documents that Jesus attended the synagogues on Sabbath (Matt. 12:9; Luke 13:10; 6:6; Mark 6:2).

Jesus Christ the founder of Christianity is the great example of every Christian. What He did they are supposed to do. Notice how plain the Bible makes this: "Christ also suffered for us, leaving us an *example*, that ye should *follow his steps*" (1 Peter 2:21). "He that saith he abideth in him ought himself also so to walk, *even as he* [Christ] *walked*" (1 John 2:6). Since Christ is our example and He kept the seventh-day Sabbath, who dare aspire to the "scorner's seat and hurl the cynic's ban" and accuse anyone who follows the example of God Himself (Gen. 2:1-3) and the Son of God Himself (Luke 4:16) in keeping the very Sabbath day which They kept?

25. Because Jesus Christ the Son of God *kept the Sabbath after* the cross.

It is a matter of common knowledge that after the crucifixion, Jesus *rested* in the grave. God *rested* on the seventh day at Creation, and Jesus, the Son of God, *rested* on the seventh day at redemption. Both in life and death Jesus honored the Sabbath.

- He lay there *before the Sabbath* (Mark 15:42-47; Luke 23:52-56).
- He remained there until *after the Sabbath was past* (Matt. 28:1; Mark 16:1; Luke 24:1, 6).

Christ's life climaxed in keeping the Sabbath. It was His custom to keep it all His life, and it was the last thing He did before He arose from the grave and went to His Father. Since it was the last thing that Christ did, if it is the last thing we ever do, we should keep the Sabbath.

Christ, while on earth, always kept the seventh-day Sabbath. It was His custom to do so. His first sermon was on the Sabbath. During the record of His life, we have no mention of any other day but the seventh as the Sabbath.

It seems very significant that Jesus, during three years of instructing His disciples, often discussed the Sabbath with them and freed it from its false burdens, making it a day of rest rather than a day of arrest. Never once in His instruction did He allude to any change of the Sabbath to Sunday. Moreover, there is not the slightest intimation of any change during the forty days after His resurrection. There is not a hint in the whole New Testament to even suggest the sanctity of any day besides the seventh-day Sabbath. Where the Bible is silent human beings ought to be silent.

It is strange that some would endeavor to change the Sabbath day after the death of Jesus since the worst kind of fraud and forgery is that which changes a person's will after they die.

God has given man a memorial of Christ's death and resurrection. We should seek to commemorate the death and resurrection of our Lord in the way of *His own appointing*, namely, by means of the Lord's supper and baptism. The Lord's supper was given by Christ Himself to be a memorial of His death (1 Cor. 11:26); and the sacred rite of baptism was given to commemorate His resurrection (Col. 2:12; Rom. 6:3-5). Baptism, then, and not Sunday or any other day, is the Bible memorial of Christ's resurrection. Since we are plainly told not to add or diminish from the Word of God (Deut. 4:2; Prov. 30:6; Rev. 22:18), it seems that all Christians would want to honor Christ's resurrection the way He wanted us to do so, not by a day, but by an institution—the ordinance of baptism.

26. Because Jesus Christ the Son of God *commanded* the keeping of the Sabbath *after* the cross.

Those who have the erroneous notion that Sunday should be kept after the cross may be sincere, but they are mistaken. While Jesus left no command or example for the observance of Sunday, He did leave solid evidence, command, and example for the observance of the seventh-day Sabbath. Here is the Bible proof:

Christ's Example:

"As his *custom was*, he [Jesus] went into the synagogue [church] on the sabbath day" (Luke 4:16).

Christ's Command:

He that said "*go ye*" also said "*pray ye.*" "Pray ye that your flight be not in the winter, *neither on the sabbath day*" (Matt. 24:20).

Christ's Command Obeyed:

"They ... rested the sabbath day according to the *commandment*" (Luke 23:56).

Why did Jesus say "neither on the Sabbath day"? Because He recognized and stressed the *sanctity* of the *Sabbath* with its keeping even at the time of the destruction of Jerusalem, AD 70, almost forty years *after* the *cross*. This clears the air of any fog that might have settled over the minds of some who question whether Christ commanded the keeping of the Sabbath after the cross.

27. Because Christ's followers kept the Sabbath *after* the cross.

It is highly significant that the Bible records the observance of the Sabbath by the followers of Christ after the death of Christ on the cross. If anyone ought to know about the proper Sabbath, it should be those who were instructed by Christ Himself. He kept it while He was with them, and they kept it when He left them:

"They returned, and prepared spices and ointments; and *rested* the sabbath day according to the commandment" (Luke 23:56).

As much as they loved Jesus, they did not desecrate the Sabbath even for Him (Luke 23:52-56; 24:1; Mark 15:42-47; 16:1). Another notable feature about it all is that Christ was with them for more than a month after His resurrection and nowhere or in no place do we find any hint of His changing the Sabbath or of His correction for their keeping of the Sabbath after He died.

28. **Because Paul, the greatest writer of the New Testament who lived *after* the cross, not only *kept* the Sabbath but *preached* on it.**

The fact is irrefutable that Paul's lifelong manner or custom was to keep the very seventh-day Sabbath that God kept at Creation and Jesus kept at redemption:

"And Paul, as his *manner was*, went in unto them, and three *sabbath days* reasoned with them out of the scriptures" (Acts 17:2).

Another very striking proof of Paul's observance of the Sabbath is found in Acts 18:4 where it states: "And he [Paul] reasoned in the synagogue [church] *every sabbath.*"

The Bible says Paul knew "the *doctrine of the Lord*" (Acts 13:12), and in the same chapter he *preached it*: "Preached to them the next *sabbath*" (Acts 13:42).

The following verses also show Paul keeping and preaching on the Sabbath: Acts 13:14, 44; 16:13.

Those who contend that nobody but Jews kept the Sabbath are parting company with the facts given in the Bible. Notice the textual evidence showing others besides Jews keeping the Sabbath:

"And when the *Jews* were gone out of the synagogue, the *Gentiles* besought that these words might be preached to them the next *sabbath....* And when the *Gentiles heard this,* they were glad" (Acts 13:42, 48).

According to the above scripture, the Gentiles asked Paul to meet with them on *Sabbath*. No other day is mentioned. Paul did not change the appointment because the Bible documents that the next Sabbath "the Gentiles heard." This provides sufficient evidence to prove that Paul preached to a non-Jewish audience on a Sabbath by their own appointment: "And he [Paul] reasoned in the synagogue *every sabbath*, and persuaded the Jews and the Greeks" (Acts 18:4).

With the above evidence at hand showing Gentiles and Greeks keeping the Sabbath, the theory that only Jews kept it has gone into hopeless bankruptcy.

29. Because the *apostolic church* kept the Sabbath *after* the cross.

Anyone who thinks the Bible teaches that any other day besides the seventh day was observed as the Sabbath after the cross is asked to examine carefully the following texts:

Texts	Church	Date	Number of Meetings
Acts 13:14, 42-44	Antioch	AD 45	2
Acts 16:12, 13	Philippi	AD 53	1
Acts 17:1, 2	Thessalonica	AD 53	3
Acts 18:1-4, 11	Corinth	AD 54	78

This list documents a total of eighty-four meetings on Sabbath. So we can easily see that nothing is more certified than the fact that the apostolic church kept the Sabbath after the cross.

30. Because the Sabbath has been kept by God's faithful all through the centuries from the time of the apostolic church to the present time.

It is a fact, obvious to any student of history, and the proofs are plentiful to furnish substantial evidence that there have always been faithful seventh-day Sabbathkeepers from the time of Christ to the present age:

AD 75—Flavius Josephus
"For there is not any city of the Grecians, nor any of the barbarians, nor any nation whatsoever, whether our custom of resting on *the seventh day* hath not come" (Flavius Josephus, *The Works of Flavius Josephus*, p. 925; italics added)

AD 250—Origen, Bishop of Alexandria
"Let us therefore no longer keep the Sabbath after Jewish manner ... But let every one of you *keep the Sabbath* after spiritual manner, rejoicing in meditation on the law"(*Epistle to the Magnesians*, chap. IX; italics added).

AD 350—Athanasius
"We are assembled on the day of the *Sabbath*, not because we are infected with Judaism ... but we approach the *Sabbath* to adore Christ, the Lord of the Sabbath" (John Nevins Andrews, *History of the Sabbath and the First Day of the Week,* p. 470; italics added).

AD 400—Augustine
"On this day, which is the *Sabbath*, mostly those are accustomed to meet who are desirous of the word of God" (Augustine's Sermon, 128, tom. 7, p. 629; italics added).

AD 450—Socrates
"Almost all of the churches throughout the world celebrate the sacred mysteries on the *Sabbath* of every week" (Socrates, book V, chap. 22; italics added).

AD 590—Pope Gregory I:
"It has come to my ears that certain men of perverse spirit have sown among you some things that are wrong and opposed to holy faith, so as to forbid any work being done on the Sabbath day" (*Nicene and Post-Nicene Fathers of the Christian Church*, vol. 13, book 13, epist. I, p. 336).

AD 791—Council of Triau (Italy)
"Further, when speaking of that *Sabbath* which the Jews observe, that last day of the week, and which also our peasants observe" (13th Canon of the Council of Triau; italics added).

Eleventh-century—Scotland
"They worked on Sunday, but kept Saturday in a sabbatical manner" (*A History of Scotland from the Roman Occupation,* vol. 1, p. 96).

Fourteenth-century—Abyssinia
"It is not, therefore, in imitation of the Jews, but in obedience to Christ and His holy apostles, that we observe that day [Sabbath]" (Michael Geddes, *Church History of Ethiopia,* pp. 87, 88; reason for keeping Sabbath given by Abyssinian legate at the court of Lisbon in 1534).

AD 1576—Waldenses
"They were called Insabbatati, not because they were circumcised, but because they kept the *Sabbath* according to the Jewish law" (*Deutsche Biographie*, vol. IX, art. "Goldast.," p. 327; italics added).

AD 1653—Goa, India
"They keep Saturday holy, nor esteem the Saturday fast lawful, but on Easter even. They have solemn service on Saturdays"

(John Nevins Andrews, *History of the Sabbath and the First Day of the Week*, p. 569).

AD 1665—Sianfu, China
Stone tablets were unearthed dating before the eighth-century: "On the *seventh day* we offer sacrifice, after having purified our hearts and received absolution for our sins" (*ibid.*, p. 565).

AD 1738—Count Nicolaus von Zinzendorf
He was the founder and the first bishop of the Moravian church. "The days which we keep are Sunday as the Lord's resurrection day, and the *Sabbath* or the *real rest day of our Lord*" (*ibid.*, p. 753; italics added).

AD 1844—Ellen G. White
"In the autumn of 1846 we began to observe the Bible Sabbath, and to teach and defend it" (*Testimonies for the Church*, vol. 1, p. 75).

31. 31.Because God's faithful church in these last days before He comes will keep the commandments of God, which contain the seventh-day Sabbath.

"And the dragon [Satan, cf. Rev. 20:2] was wroth with the woman [God's church, cf. Jer. 6:2; 2 Cor. 11:2], and went to make war with the remnant [last or remaining part, cf. Ex. 26:12] of her seed, which *keep the commandments* [Ten Commandments, cf. Matt. 19:17-19] of God" (Rev. 12:17; see also 14:12).

32. Because the other churches say I'm right in keeping the seventh-day Sabbath.

A man may rub his eyes in amazement when he sees the following quotations to support my thirty-five reasons. These have been selected from the writings of reputable Sunday-keeping authors. While I have the deepest veneration for their sincerity, I, with Job, cannot help but say, "Thine own mouth condemneth thee, and not I: yea, thine own lips testify against thee" (Job 15:6).

Lutheran
"The observance of the Lord's day [Sunday] is founded not on any command of God, but on the authority of the church" (*Augsburg Confession of Faith*, as quoted in the Catholic Sabbath Manual, part 2, chap. 1, sec. 10).

Episcopal
"We have made the change from the seventh day to the first day, from Saturday to Sunday, on the authority of the one holy Catholic, Apostolic Church of Christ" (Bishop Seymour, *Why We Keep Sunday*).

Methodist
"It is true there is no positive command for infant baptism, … nor is there any for keeping holy the first day of the week" (M. E., *Theological Compendium*, p. 103).

Baptist
"There was and is a commandment to keep holy the Sabbath day, but that Sabbath day was not Sunday…. There is no Scriptural evidence of the change of the Sabbath institution from the seventh to the first day of the week" (Edward T. Hiscox, D.D., *The Baptist Church Manual*).

Presbyterian
"The Christian Sabbath [Sunday] is not in the Scripture, and was not by the primitive church called the Sabbath" (*Dwight's Theology*, vol. IV, p. 401).

Congregational
"There is no command in the Bible, requiring us to observe the first day of the week as the Christian Sabbath" (Orin Fowler, *Mode and Subjects of Baptism*, p. 93).

Christian
"The first day of the week is commonly called the Sabbath. This is a mistake. The Sabbath of the Bible was the day just preceding the first day of the week. The first day of the week is never called the Sabbath anywhere in the entire Scriptures. It is also an error to talk about the change of the Sabbath. There never was any change of the Sabbath from Saturday to Sunday. There is not at any place in the Bible any intimation of such a change" (*First Day Observance*, pp. 17-19).

Catholic
James Cardinal Gibbons hit the nail on the head in the following statement. In this statement he is splendidly right. "But you may read the Bible from Genesis to Revelation, and you will not find a single line authorizing the sanctification of Sunday. The Scriptures enforce the religious observance of Saturday, a day which we never sanctify" (*Faith of Our Fathers*, pp. 111, 112).

"If the Bible is the only guide for the Christian, then the Seventh Day Adventist is *right* in observing the Saturday with the Jew" (Bertrand L. Conway, *The Question-Box Answers*, p. 254).

33. Because the change of the calendar has not altered or lost the seventh-day Sabbath.

What higher authority could we cite than the royal astronomer of England and the director of the U.S. Naval Observatory? Notice what these authorities state concerning the change of the calendar and the altering of the weekly cycle:

"As far as I know, in the various changes of the Calendar there has been no change in the seven day rota of the week" (Frank W. Dyson, astronomer royal, Royal Observatory, Greenwich, London, 1932).

"We have had occasion to investigate the results on the works of specialists in chronology and we have never found one of them that has ever had the slightest doubt about the continuity of the weekly cycle since long before the Christian era.... There has been no change in our calendar in past centuries that has affected in any way the cycle of the week" (James Robertson, director American Ephemeris, U.S. Naval Observatory).

Showing the Change From the Julian to the Gregorian Calendar

1582 OCTOBER 1582

S	M	T	W	T	F	S
	1	2	3	4	15	16
17	18	19	20	21	22	23
24	25	26	27	28	29	30
31						

"The change from old style to new style did not interfere in any way with the free-running week. The change was made on Friday, October 5, 1582. Ten days were made up by calling the

5th of October the 15th of October. This is all that was done."

The various changes of the calendar affected the days of the month and not the days of the week, hence no time has been lost. Consequently the *Sabbath day* is still the *seventh day* of the week or *Saturday*.

34. Because keeping the commandments, which includes the Sabbath, will be a passport into heaven.

A passport is something that gives a person a *right* to go somewhere. The commandment *keepers* and *doers* have the *right* to enter into the city of God, which is in heaven (Gal. 4:26).

"Blessed are they that *do* his commandments, that they may have *right* to the tree of life, and may enter in through the gates into the city" (Rev. 22:14).

It is admitted that no one can *do* this in his/her own strength but they can *do* it *through Christ*: "I can *do* all things *through Christ* which strengtheneth me" (Phil. 4:13).

35. Because the Sabbath will be *kept in heaven* by *all flesh*.

This reason has the ring of finality in it because it leads to the inevitable conclusion that the Sabbath will be kept in heaven by *all*—Jew as well as Gentile. Every person that gets to heaven will keep the Sabbath there. Here is the Bible proof:

"For as the *new* heavens and the *new* earth, which I will make, shall remain before me, saith the LORD, so shall your seed and your name remain. And *it shall come to pass*, that from one new moon to another [cf. Rev. 22:2], and from one *sabbath* to another, shall *all* flesh come to worship before me, saith the LORD" (Isa. 66:22, 23).

Since the seventh-day Sabbath was in the world before sin came, it will be in the world when sin is gone (Gen. 2:1-3; Isa. 66:22, 23). Consequently, the incident of sin in the history of our world has not, does not, and will not make void the eternal claims of the seventh-day as the Sabbath on this earth.

Conclusion

The Bible conclusion and the final analysis of the Sabbath lead us to the ultimate fact that beyond all doubt or question of uncertainty the seventh day (Saturday) is the *true Bible Sabbath* and all *true* Christians ought to keep it. Notice the Bible conclusion:

"There remaineth *therefore* a rest [keeping of a *Sabbath*] to the people of God…. Let us labour *therefore* to enter into *that rest*, lest any man fall after the same example of unbelief" (Heb. 4:9, 11).

"Let us hear the *conclusion* of the *whole matter*: Fear God, and *keep his commandments* [including the seventh-day Sabbath]: for this is the *whole* duty of man" (Eccl. 12:13).

Since *God* kept the seventh-day Sabbath at *Creation* and commanded man to keep it (Gen. 2:1-3; Ex. 20:8-11);

Since *Christ* kept it at *redemption* and commanded man to keep it (Luke 4:16; Matt. 24:20; 28:1);

Since *all the saints* will keep it in heaven (Isa. 66:22, 23);

If we are going to keep it there, why not here?

If we are going to keep it then, why not now?

> "Oh when, thou city of my God,
> Shall I thy courts ascend,
> Where congregations ne'er break up,
> And Sabbaths have no end" (author unknown).

We invite you to view the complete
selection of titles we publish at:

www.TEACHServices.com

Scan with your mobile
device to go directly
to our website.

Please write or email us your praises, reactions, or
thoughts about this or any other book we publish at:

TEACH Services, Inc.
P U B L I S H I N G
www.TEACHServices.com

P.O. Box 954
Ringgold, GA 30736

info@TEACHServices.com

TEACH Services, Inc., titles may be purchased in bulk for
educational, business, fund-raising, or sales promotional use.
For information, please e-mail:

BulkSales@TEACHServices.com

Finally, if you are interested in seeing
your own book in print, please contact us at

publishing@TEACHServices.com

We would be happy to review your manuscript for free.

www.ingramcontent.com/pod-product-compliance
Lightning Source LLC
LaVergne TN
LVHW021548080426
835509LV00019B/2909

*9 7 8 1 5 7 2 5 8 7 1 7 5 *